One Anothering™

Choosing each other
in a politically divided world

THIS BOOK BELONGS TO

_____

DATE

_____

OneAnothering.com

ColossianForum.org

The Colossian Forum™

© 2024 by The Colossian Forum

Design: Crowe X-Lab

All rights reserved.

ISBN 979-8-3302-8179-4

No part of this publication may be reproduced, distributed, or transmitted in any form or by any means, including photo-copying, recording, or other electronic or mechanical methods, without the prior written permission of The Colossian Forum.

All Scripture is taken from the NIV Bible.

One Anothering™

Choosing each other
in a politically divided world

God calls us to love one another.

GROUP DISCUSSION GOAL
Participate in politics with a Kingdom posture that helps us to love one another, even as our differences remain.

INTRO

Welcome to "One Anothering," a journey toward a deeper love of God and one another. Through this group discussion guide, you'll begin to discover that every conversation—even the challenging ones about politics—is an opportunity to grow in the fruit of the Spirit. This discussion guide is designed to help you cultivate a mindset and practices to engage these tough topics in a way that brings us closer to God and each other.

The term "one another" comes from the Greek word *allelon,* which appears 100 times in the New Testament. These verses, such as Jesus' command in John 13: "A new command I give you: Love one another. As I have loved you, so you must love one another. By this, everyone will know that you are my disciples, if you love one another," guide us in building relationships marked by Christ's love.

Our deep hope is that by practicing "One Anothering," you will be empowered to embody these Christlike qualities in your everyday interactions. Each chapter concludes with practical steps to apply what you've learned, encouraging you to live out your faith in real-world conversations.

We know this journey won't be perfect. Yet, by rooting ourselves in Christ, we can confidently face political differences, trusting that even our imperfect efforts will point others toward the Kingdom of God.

How to use this book

This discussion guide is about loving one another more fully and deeply—through politics. We'll do this by cultivating a posture (or way of being) that reflects Christ.

How do we cultivate a different way of being? In the first several sessions, we'll examine our mindsets (or our ways of thinking) and practice habits to bring our thinking more fully into alignment with Christ. Then we'll turn to more specific aspects of a Christlike posture and practice spiritual and interpersonal habits that invite the Holy Spirit in to form our hearts, minds, and actions.

Shifting our **posture** requires reforming both our **mindsets** and our **habits**.

POSTURE: Way of being

MINDSET: Way of thinking

HABIT: Way of interacting

The 8-week sessions:

	SESSION 1	SESSION 2	SESSION 3	SESSION 4
FROM	Polarized Politics	Scarcity	Contempt	Cocooning & Combat
	Examine our Political Formation	Practice Surrender	Behold Others	Hold Compassion & Conviction Together
TO	Kingdom Politics	Abundance	Love	Covenantal Communication
	Pg. 10	Pg. 20	Pg. 30	Pg. 40

FACILITATING A GROUP?

Facilitators can find additional resources and videos at *OneAnothering.com*

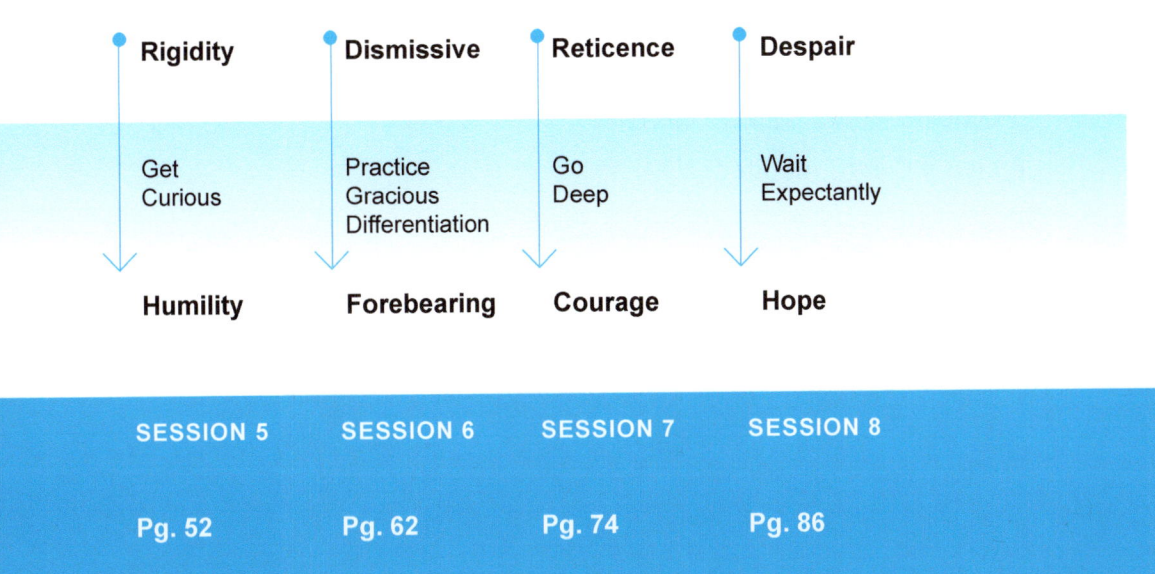

Rigidity	Dismissive	Reticence	Despair
Get Curious	Practice Gracious Differentiation	Go Deep	Wait Expectantly
Humility	**Forebearing**	**Courage**	**Hope**
SESSION 5	SESSION 6	SESSION 7	SESSION 8
Pg. 52	Pg. 62	Pg. 74	Pg. 86

Polarized Politics — Scarcity — Contempt — Cocooning & Combat — Rigidity — Dismissive — Reticence — Despair

Kingdom Politics — Abundance — Love — Covenantal Communication — Humility — Forebearing — Courage — Hope

SESSION 1
From Polarized Politics to Kingdom Politics

OVERVIEW

In this introductory session, we contrast polarized politics with Kingdom Politics and consider the ways that our early experiences have shaped our political postures, mindsets, and habits.

OUTLINE

1 Introduction (6 minutes)	11
2 Opening Prayer: Palms Down, Palms Up (5 minutes)	12
3 From Polarized Politics to Kingdom Politics (20+ minutes)	14
4 Examine our Political Formation (25+ minutes)	16
5 Closing Prayer (2 minutes)	18
6 Live it Out (2 minutes)	19

The times suggested here assume your group is meeting for an hour. We highly suggest meeting for 90 minutes if possible. If you have more than 60 minutes, we suggest extending the time in the sections that your group connects with best. We imagine that the parts of this session marked with the + sign above may benefit from additional time, if possible. If your group has not met together previously, you will also need to set aside a bit more time for brief introductions in the first part of this session.

①

Introduction   *6 minutes*

If your group has not met together previously, we suggest briefly introducing yourselves at this point, providing basic information relevant to your group's context (for example, how long you have been at your church or why you joined the group). It is important to keep these introductions brief. The fourth part of this session will provide you with the chance to get to know one another more deeply.

Welcome

The video explains that this series will help us embody a Christ-like way of being in this political moment.

FROM TANNER SMITH AND ASHLEE EILAND

oneanothering.com/politicswelcome | 3:36

Some Christian traditions use Reign of God language and some use Kingdom language to refer to the same idea. We use Kingdom language because it is more common across Christian traditions. Groups who prefer Reign of God language can make substitutions throughout.

SESSION 1 | 11

2

Opening Prayer: Palms Down, Palms Up *5 minutes*

FACILITATOR As we begin our time together each session, we will enter prayer. To start this session, we will engage in a prayer practice called Palms Down, Palms Up. The practice invites us to surrender to God and receive from God.

Let's begin by voicing together these words from Psalm 139:

GROUP **Search me, God, and know my heart;***
test me and know my anxious thoughts.
See if there is any offensive way in me,
and lead me in the way everlasting. (Psalm 139:23-24)

FACILITATOR Let's start by placing our palms down, in an emptying posture. Placing our palms down reflects our desire to turn over any concerns we may have to God. As we pray, surrender what we usually grasp and cling to.

Let's pray aloud, naming things that we wish to release as we begin our time together as a group. For example, "Lord, I surrender my anxiety about talking about politics." "I release my fear of silence to you."

Whatever weighs on our minds or hearts or is a concern, let's release it to God.

Allow space for spoken or silent prayers

Palms Down, Palms Up originally comes from Richard Foster's *Celebration of Discipline*. This version was adapted by Ruth Haley Barton in *Invitation to Silence and Solitude*.

* We use bold font throughout to indicate items that the group should say together.

FACILITATOR Now let's place our palms up, in a receiving posture. Placing our palms up is a symbol of our desire to receive from God.

Let's pray aloud, asking God to provide for us. For example, "Lord, give me peace about this conversation." "Lord, give us hope for how we might participate in politics." Whatever we need, let's ask God to provide it.

Allow space for spoken or silent prayers

Let's close by voicing together these words from Psalm 139:

GROUP **You have searched me, Lord, and you know me.** (Psalm 139:1)
Amen.

3

From Polarized Politics to Kingdom Politics   *20 minutes*

Next, we will watch a video that introduces the central posture shift from polarized politics to Kingdom Politics that is at the heart of One Anothering. This video lays the foundation for the work you will be engaging in throughout this series, as each session will invite you to continue to shift your posture, mindsets, and habits.

From Polarized Politics to Kingdom Politics

FROM ASHLEE EILAND

oneanothering.com/politics1 | 4:35

KEY IDEAS IN THE VIDEO

As Christians, we cannot simply cocoon, sheltering ourselves completely or even just avoiding conversations about politics. This small group series invites us to participate in politics with a Kingdom posture that helps us to love one another, even as our differences remain.

Dwelling in God's Kingdom requires shifting our postures to align with God's ways. Shifting our postures requires re-forming both our mindsets and our habits.

A Kingdom posture is made possible when we remain rooted in Christ, the true vine (John 12:1-8).

POSTURE		MINDSET		HABITS
Way of being	=	Way of thinking	+	Ways of interacting

- **Polarized Politics**: Participating in politics in ways that reflect a lack of Christian discipleship; for example, enacting love for neighbor and hate for enemies

HABIT — Examine our Political Formation

- **Kingdom Politics**: Participating in politics in ways that reflect discipleship in Christ; for example, enacting Jesus' command to love your enemies and pray for those who persecute you (Matthew 5:43-44)

DISCUSSION

Process the video by discussing the following questions. We suggest that you first discuss in groups of 2 or 3 for about five minutes and then share thoughts with the whole group for about ten minutes.

1. What in the video struck me?

2. What habits help me remain rooted in Jesus, the true vine? What habits cut me off from the true vine?

3. Galatians 5:22 tells us that "the fruit of the Spirit is love, joy, peace, patience, kindness, goodness, faithfulness, gentleness and self-control."

   - Which of these is most challenging in political conflict? What makes it hard?

   - Which is most helpful in political conflict? Why?

(4)

Examine our Political Formation   *25 minutes*

In order to get acquainted and consider how our early experiences shaped our political postures, mindsets, and habits, we will introduce ourselves by sharing a memorable message from our childhoods that stands out related to politics. Memorable messages are 'sticky' messages that influenced our belief systems and behaviors.

We will take a few minutes of silence to consider what we each want to share with the group about this question:

**Thinking back to my childhood,
what memorable message stands out about politics?**

Let's share our memorable messages, starting with one person and then going around the circle, giving each person a chance to briefly share (in a sentence not a paragraph). Please resist the temptation to affirm, comment, or build on each other's ideas in order to allow each person's experience to be shared and received as equally relevant and valuable.

DISCUSSION

After everyone has shared, discuss these questions:

1. What similarities and differences do we notice among our experiences?

2. Memorable messages both reflect and shape our postures, mindsets, and habits. For example, the memorable message that, "We have to do whatever it takes politically to get what is best for us," may reflect a fearful posture, a scarcity mindset that believes that there is not enough to go around and may result in habits of engaging political differences in ways that are anxious.

   What postures, mindsets, or habits do our memorable messages reflect or encourage?

3. How does examining these messages help us understand how our early life experiences shape our political postures, mindsets, and/or habits? Have they encouraged our participation in polarized politics or Kingdom politics—or perhaps a bit of both?

Closing Prayer

Come, Holy Spirit, Come.
Come as the wind, and cleanse.
Come as the fire, and burn.
Come as the water, and refresh.
Convict; Convert; Consecrate
Until we are wholly thine. Amen.

(Adapted from Eric Milner-White)

Live it Out *2 minutes*

Briefly review this invitation to live it out before next session.

EXAMINING MY CONFLICT FORMATION

From an early age, we each learned—often through observation and experience—the value of conflict and how it should look and sound. In this exercise, you will reflect on those early lessons and how they have shaped your habits for engaging both conflict and political differences.

Reflect on the questions below in light of three childhood contexts:
- The family I grew up in
- An organization in which I participated (e.g., church or civic group)
- The region where I grew up

1. What did I learn from each context about how conflict should be engaged?

2. What did I learn from each context about how political differences should be engaged?

3. How have those lessons shaped my habits for responding to conflict and political differences?

4. Which habits do I wish to carry with me? Which habits do I wish to leave behind?

SESSION 2
From Scarcity to Abundance

OVERVIEW

In this session, we will consider how to reorient from scarcity to abundance and will practice the habit of surrender.

OUTLINE

1 Opening Prayer (6 minutes)	21
2 Follow Up: Conflict Formation Stories (30+ minutes)	22
3 From Scarcity to Abundance (20+ minutes)	24
4 Closing Prayer (2 minutes)	27
6 Live it Out (2 minutes)	28

① Opening Prayer *6 minutes*

Psalm 23 is a psalm all about abundance. As we read this together, let's listen for messages about abundance: Where does David's abundance mindset come through in these words?

> **The Lord is my shepherd,
> I lack nothing.
> He makes me lie down
> in green pastures,
> he leads me beside
> quiet waters,
> he refreshes my soul.
> He guides me along
> the right paths
> for his name's sake.
> Even though I walk
> through the darkest valley,
> I will fear no evil,
> for you are with me;
> your rod and your staff,
> they comfort me.
> You prepare a table before me
> in the presence of my enemies.
> You anoint my head with oil;
> my cup overflows.
> Surely your goodness
> and love will follow me
> all the days of my life,
> and I will dwell in the
> house of the Lord forever.**

What word or phrase struck you as we read Psalm 23?
Offer your word or phrase aloud.

Allow space for the sharing of words or phrases.

LET'S PRAY TOGETHER

**Good Shepherd,
Thank you for providing all that we need.
Help us to follow you and inhabit your ways.**

Amen

2

Follow Up: Conflict Formation Stories *30 minutes*

From an early age, we each learned—often through observation and experience —the value of conflict and how it should look and sound. We were all undoubtedly formed in significant ways by the families who raised us, organizations we participated in, and where we grew up.

In the first half of this session, we will each share our reflections about how **one** of those contexts has shaped our mindsets and habits in relation to conflict and political differences, as well as which mindsets and habits we want to carry with us and leave behind.

Let's share our formation stories, starting with one person and then going around the circle. In order to allow each person's experience to be shared and received as equally relevant and valuable, please resist the temptation to chime in, comment, or build on one other's stories.

As we listen to each other's formation stories, we will come to know and understand each other more deeply. Listening to one another's stories can also help us each gain clarity on our own experience of formation.

DISCUSSION

After sharing our formation stories, we will take a few minutes to discuss these questions:

1. What did you notice as you listened to one another's formation stories?

2. How might understanding our conflict formation stories help us as we seek to re-form our political postures?

3

From Scarcity to Abundance

20 minutes

This video introduces a shift from a scarcity to abundance mindset that will help us participate in politics with a Kingdom posture that reflects love for one another, even as our differences remain.

 From Scarcity to Abundance

FROM TANNER SMITH

oneanothering.com/politics2 | 4:24

KEY IDEAS IN THE VIDEO

Jesus invites us to stop treating others like a threat and instead trust that God is doing something bigger and more beautiful than we are aware. If we run after God's Kingdom and God's right ways of living, everything else will fall into place.

When we hold a scarcity mindset, we can easily fall into the habit of trying to control people and situations in order to create outcomes that serve our individual interests or the interests of our group.

Jesus offers us a new mindset of abundance in the Sermon on the Mount. An abundance mindset moves us from seeking power over others to surrendering to God's will by loving God, neighbor, and enemy.

Kingdom ways are not something we can achieve through willpower—they are a way of being that we embrace because of the movement of the Holy Spirit within us, through us, around us, and in the lives of people we disagree with.

- **Scarcity** — Belief that there isn't enough to go around

HABIT — Practice Surrender

- **Abundance** — Belief that God is doing more than we are aware

DISCUSSION

To contrast scarcity and abundance mindsets, review the statements. We suggest you read through the list aloud, alternating between someone serving as the voice of scarcity and another serving as the voice of abundance.

SCARCITY MINDSET Belief that there is not enough to go around	ABUNDANCE MINDSET Belief that God is doing more than we are aware
Politics is so corrupt. I will not have anything to do with it.	I am curious how God is at work in the midst of our flawed political system. And I wonder how God might be calling me to get involved.
There's no point in arguing about politics. All we ever do is hurt each other without solving anything.	This is hard, but I believe God can work in me, in us, and in the world through this process.
To each one's own.	I wonder what God might be teaching me through these differences.
I don't like either candidate so I am not voting.	Even though I have concerns about the candidates, I will vote for the one whose values best reflect mine.
We know what's best for the country and they don't. They are a lost cause.	While I disagree with [candidate] on many things, I am curious to see it the way that they do and am eager to discover areas where we can work together.
There are only two options, so we both can't get what we want.	I wonder if there are some creative solutions other than the two we have come up with so far. I think if we keep talking, we might be able to come up with something workable for both of us.

SESSION 2 | 25

DISCUSSION

Continue contrasting scarcity and abundance mindsets by discussing the questions below:

1. Thinking back to our formation stories, what reflections of scarcity or abundance do we recognize?

2. In our current political context, when have you seen individuals or groups responding out of a scarcity mindset by seeking control?

3. In our current political context, when have you seen individuals or groups responding out of an abundance mindset and practicing surrender?

4. What would have to be true for you to hold an abundance mindset? What would you need to let go of (surrender) to live into an abundance mindset?

(4)

Closing Prayer   *2 minutes*

FACILITATOR God, we find ourselves stuck in a political story that, if believed, makes us captives.

GROUP **But you, LORD, have set us free.**

Take our freedom, our memory, our understanding, our whole will,

And lead us to surrender to your Spirit's guiding love.

All that we are, and all that we have are a gift from you.

**May we give thanks to you,
With our mouths,
With our actions,
With our resources.**

**Lead us to gratitude and respect for those who serve in government.
Keep us mindful that, while they are allowed to lead:**

**You alone provide and sustain
You alone deliver lasting peace
You alone bring true joy**

Our hearts are restless until we find our rest in you.

Amen.

(5)

Live it Out

2 minutes

ABUNDANCE AND SCARCITY MINDSETS
Pay attention this week:

When do you notice that you are operating out of a scarcity mindset?
When do you notice that you are operating out of an abundance mindset?

How does each look, feel, and sound?

Live in harmony with one another.

Romans 12:16

SESSION 3
From Contempt to Love

OVERVIEW

In this session, we will consider the need to reorient our mindsets from contempt to love in order to hold a Kingdom posture in the midst of political polarization. We will introduce the habit of beholding others as a way to practice loving neighbors who hold different political views than our own.

OUTLINE

1 Opening Prayer (3 minutes)	31
2 Follow Up: Abundance and Scarcity Mindsets (10 minutes)	32
3 From Contempt to Love (10+ minutes)	34
4 Being Seen with the Eyes of Love (30+ minutes)	36
5 Closing Prayer: Give Us New Eyes (6 minutes)	38
6 Live it Out (1 minute)	39

① Opening Prayer *3 minutes*

FACILITATOR And so are we gathered here, uniquely in all of history, we particular people in this singular time and place.

GROUP **Accomplish your purposes among us, O God.**

FACILITATOR Tune our hearts to the voice of your Spirit.

GROUP **Wake us to be present to you and to one another in these shared hours we are given.**

FACILITATOR For it is you, O Lord, who have so gathered us from our various places,

GROUP **and you alone who know our hearts and our needs.**

FACILITATOR Among us are some who arrive anxious, some who are lonely, some who suffer pain or sorrow.

GROUP **May we in our joys find grace to enter the sorrows of others.**

FACILITATOR Among us are some who arrive rejoicing, hearts made light by good news, good health, glad anticipation.

GROUP **May we in our sorrows find grace to embrace the joys of others.**

FACILITATOR Let us prize these moments and care for one another deeply. For each of us, and our relationships to one another, are precious and fleeting.

GROUP **Breathe upon our gathering, O Spirit of God.**

FACILITATOR Grant each of us a place to humbly receive and to faithfully serve, that we might know in this brief gathering a foretaste of that greater communion yet to come.

GROUP **O Father, enlarge our hearts.**

FACILITATOR O Spirit, expand our vision.

GROUP **O Christ, establish your reign among us.**

FACILITATOR Be at work even now, O Lord. May your will, in us, in these hours, be accomplished.

GROUP **Amen.**

Liturgy from Every Moment Holy, Vol I by Douglas Kaine McKelvey

(2)

Follow Up: Abundance & Scarcity Mindsets   *10 minutes*

Last session, we focused on making this shift:

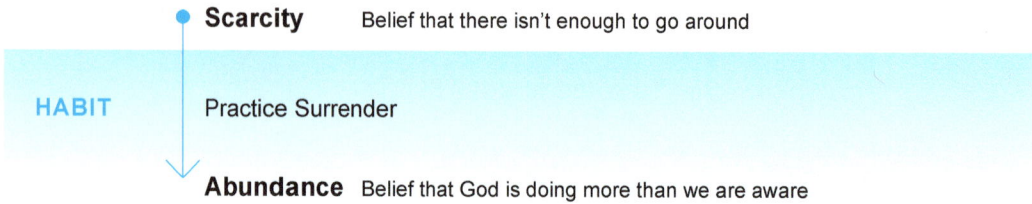

Respond to the questions below as you feel led:

DISCUSSION

What have you noticed or wondered about scarcity and abundance mindsets?

What would it look like to gently invite others to move towards abundance when they voice scarcity in relation to politics?

3

From Contempt to Love 10 minutes

This video introduces a shift from contempt to love that will help us participate in politics with a Kingdom posture that reflects love for one another, even as our differences remain.

From Contempt to Love

FROM ASHLEE EILAND

oneanothering.com/politics3 | 4:17

KEY IDEAS IN THE VIDEO

God invites us to see one another not with the eyes of contempt, but with the eyes of love.

Our current political moment is infected with a 'culture of contempt' ",a habit of seeing people who disagree with us not as merely incorrect or misguided but as worthless" (Arthur Brooks).

Reconciliation means healing what is broken, and Paul says that reconciliation starts with learning to see one another differently —"regarding no one from a worldly point of view" (2 Corinthians 5).

We need to "behold" one another. Beholding is a special kind of seeing, perhaps best summed up in the ancient Latin phrase ubi amor, ibi oculus—"where there is love, there is seeing."

We can see others with the eyes of love only because God has first seen us through the eyes of love. We can behold because God beholds us. "We love because God first loved us" (1 John 4:19).

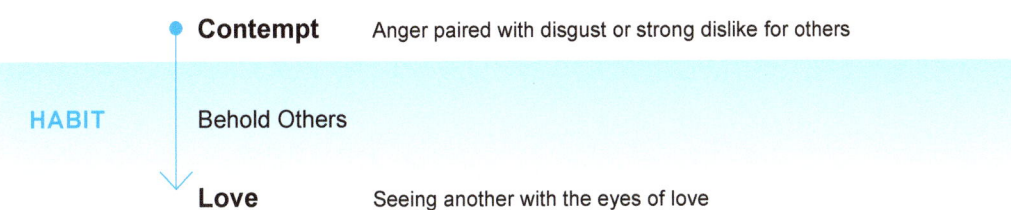

HABIT Behold Others

DISCUSSION
Process the video for five minutes by engaging the following question.

1. What struck you in the video?

BEHOLDING OTHERS
Seeing another with the eyes of love.

Reflection: Being Seen with the Eyes of Love *30 minutes*

Next, we will consider times when we have felt seen with the eyes of contempt and the eyes of love. Take five minutes to reflect individually.

1. **Being Seen with the Eyes of Contempt**
   Think of a situation in which you have felt seen with the eyes of contempt. What did it feel like? What did the other person do or not do that led you to believe that they were seeing you through the eyes of contempt? How did feeling their contempt shape your response and how you saw them?

   UBI AMOR, IBI OCULUS.
   Where there is love, there is seeing.

2. **Being Seen with the Eyes of Love**
   Now, think of a person who typically sees you with the eyes of love. How do you know? What does it feel like? What did they do or not do that shows you they behold you? How does feeling their love shape your response and how you see them?

DISCUSSION

Next, let's spend 10 minutes discussing our reflections as a group. As we do so, let's flesh out what contempt and love look like below.

SEEING WITH THE EYES OF CONTEMPT	SEEING WITH THE EYES OF LOVE

DISCUSSION

Finally, let's think about how contempt and love shape politics by discussing the following questions.

1. When have you seen contempt activated in politics? What did it look like?

2. When have you seen love activated in politics? What did it look like?

3. How might you gently invite others to move toward love when you hear or see them demonstrate contempt for one another?

5

Closing Prayer: Give Us New Eyes *6 minutes*

FACILITATOR God, from the dust of the earth you made us, breathing your life-giving breath into us. In your own image, you created us. Even now, you animate us with your Holy Spirit. Filling us with wonder and imagination, longings, and desires. You made us for love, and how quickly love can turn to fear. But there is no fear in love, and You delight in your creation. Teach us to delight in your creation, too.

So often we see with the eyes of contempt. We are suspicious, dismissive, and disdaining. God, we confess to you now some of the ways that we have viewed your creation, and one another, in ways that dehumanize and demonize.

GROUP **Forgive us, we pray:**
Allow space for spoken or silent prayers

FACILITATOR Creator, you made us in your image: Renew our vision. We willingly lay down our eyes of contempt in order that we might receive eyes of love. Holy Spirit, convict, counsel, and lead us so that loving proceeds seeing.

God, we ask you now to lead us to understanding and reverence for you and for one another.

GROUP **Redeemer, transformer of our sight, help us:**
Allow space for spoken or silent prayers

FACILITATOR Savior, seated on the Throne, we remember in this moment that you are making all things new.

GROUP **May it be so in us this day. Amen.**

(6)

Live it Out
1 minute

Briefly review this invitation to live it out before next session.

SEEING OTHERS WHEN ENGAGING POLITICS

Before the next session, pay attention when politics comes up in conversation, on social media, and while engaging media. Tune in to both your habits and the habits of others.

What habits reflect contempt for others? What habits reflect love for others?

Polarized Politics · Scarcity · Contempt · **Cocooning & Combat** · Rigidity · Dismissive · Reticence · Despair

Kingdom Politics · Abundance · Love · **Covenantal Communication** · Humility · Forebearing · Courage · Hope

SESSION 4
From Cocooning and Combat to Covenantal Communication

OVERVIEW

In this session, we will consider how a Kingdom posture requires us to shift from postures of cocooning and combat to a posture of covenantal communication. We will explore the habit of holding compassion and conviction together as reflecting a covenantal posture.

OUTLINE

1 Opening Prayer (2 minutes)	41
2 Follow Up: Contempt and Love in Political Engagement (8 minutes)	42
3 From Cocooning and Combat to Covenantal Communication (15+ minutes)	44
4 Holding Compassion and Conviction Together (30+ minutes)	46
5 Closing Prayer (4 minutes)	50
6 Live it Out (1 minute)	51

(1)

Opening Prayer *2 minutes*

FACILITATOR O Lord, our God. Form us more fully into your likeness. Use the circumstances and interactions of local and national politics to form your will in us:

GROUP **From the frustrations of politics, form forbearance.
From the uncertainties of politics, form humility.
From the struggles of the election, form courage.
From the beauties of politics, form hope.**

FACILITATOR In the name of Jesus Christ, who shows us perfect forbearance and humility and courage and hope.

GROUP **Amen.**

2

Follow Up: Contempt and Love in Political Engagement

8 minutes

Last session, we focused on making this shift:

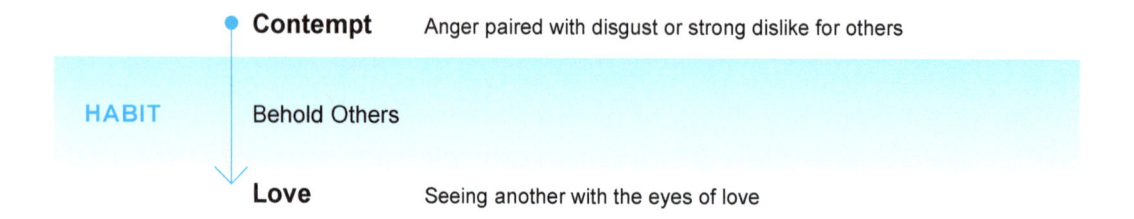

Contempt — Anger paired with disgust or strong dislike for others

HABIT — Behold Others

Love — Seeing another with the eyes of love

DISCUSSION

What did you notice by paying attention to habits reflecting both contempt and love when politics came up in conversation, on social media, and in the news?

BEHOLD OTHERS

Seeing another with the eyes of love.

Love one another.

John 13:34

3

From Cocooning and Combat to Covenantal Communication

15 minutes

This video introduces a shift toward convenantal communication that will help us participate in politics with a Kingdom posture that reflects love for one another, even as our differences remain.

From Cocooning and Combat to Covenantal Communication

FROM TANNER SMITH

oneanothering.com/politics4 | 4:42

KEY IDEAS IN THE VIDEO

Christians are called to follow the way of Christ—loving our neighbors and even our enemies—regardless of how others act.

Covenantal Communication means treating others as unique individuals created in God's image: We encounter others expectantly, open to who they are and what God is doing in them and through them.

Covenantal Communication is not merely a set of techniques but a posture, a way of being that reflects deeply rooted Christian virtues such as hope, humility, generosity, forbearance, and courage.

Covenantal communication seeks to hold compassion and conviction together. A compassionate posture beholds others as made in God's image. A convicted posture courageously and humbly pursues truth and justice.

Coccooning and Combat — Approaching others with an avoidant or defensive posture

HABIT — Hold Compassion and Conviction Together

Convenantal Communication — Approaching others with an expectant posture

	COCOONING COMMUNICATION	COMBATIVE COMMUNICATION	COVENANTAL COMMUNICATION
POSTURE	Avoidant Fearful	Defensive Adversarial	Collaborative
GOALS	Peacekeeping Comfort	Protecting Principles Winning	Peacemaking Loving God & Neighbor
MOVES	Disconnect Dodge Minimize	Dehumanize Debate Dogmatize	Behold Others Hold Compassion Conviction Together
OUTCOMES	Distance Distrust Desires of the Flesh Gal 5:19-21	Division Damage Desires of the Flesh Gal 5:19-21	Communion & Affection Christ-Life Character Fruit of the Spirit Gal 5:22-23

DISCUSSION

We suggest that you first discuss in groups of 2 or 3 for a few minutes and then share thoughts with the whole group.

1. How have you seen cocooning and combat present in your community and in politics more broadly?

2. When it comes to conflict, do you tend toward "cocoon" or "combat"? A bit of both? Or neither? Why?

3. What do you notice about covenantal communication? What do you wonder?

4

Holding Compassion and Conviction Together

30 minutes

JESUS HOLDS ALL THINGS TOGETHER *(8 minutes)*

To better understand what convenantal communication looks like, we'll look at the story of the woman accused of adultery from John 8.

As we read the story, let's imagine ourselves in the text.

> The teachers of the law and the Pharisees brought in a woman caught in adultery. They made her stand before the group and said to Jesus, "Teacher, this woman was caught in the act of adultery. In the Law, Moses commanded us to stone such women. Now what do you say?" They were using this question as a trap, in order to have a basis for accusing him.
>
> But Jesus bent down and started to write on the ground with his finger. When they kept on questioning him, he straightened up and said to them, "Let any one of you who is without sin be the first to throw a stone at her." Again, he stooped down and wrote on the ground.
>
> At this, those who heard began to go away one at a time, the older ones first, until only Jesus was left, with the woman still standing there. Jesus straightened up and asked her, "Woman, where are they? Has no one condemned you?"
>
> "No one, sir," she said. "Then neither do I condemn you," Jesus declared. "Go now and leave your life of sin."
>
> John 8:3–11

DISCUSSION

What did you notice?

What do you wonder?

How does Jesus demonstrate holding compassion and conviction together?

FOUR POSTURES FOR ENGAGING POLITICAL CONFLICT *(12 minutes)*

Now we'll consider more deeply what it looks like to hold compassion and conviction together as we engage political differences by considering four postures that combine compassion and conviction differently.

First, let's envision the four postures by imagining how they look nonverbally. As one volunteer reads the description of each quadrant below, we will have two other volunteers sit across from one another and imagine how their physical postures might look from that quadrant. Let's start with the first quadrant (lower left) and end in the fourth quadrant (upper right).

CONVICTION
Courageously and humbly pursuing truth and justice

HIGH CONVICTION, LOW COMPASSION
- Punitive
- Authoritarian
- Defensive
- Division

HIGH CONVICTION, HIGH COMPASSION
- Restorative
- Collaborative
- Covenantal
- Deep Unity

LOW CONVICTION, LOW COMPASSION
- Neglectful
- Disengaged
- Avoidant
- Apathy

LOW CONVICTION, HIGH COMPASSION
- Permissive
- Friendly
- Accommodating
- Surface Unity

COMPASSION
Beholding others as made in God's image

Adapted from Social Discipline Window (McCold and Wachtel, 2001); Managerial Grid (Blake & Mouton, 1981); Conflict Styles (Thomas-Killmann, 1974, 2007); Conflict Cultures (Gefland, et al., 2012).

Rather than asking ourselves which of the postures we hold, it is more helpful to recognize that each of us holds each posture at different times and in different contexts.

Let's consider when we are likely to show up in each posture. We will designate a corner of the room to represent each of the postures.

There are signs for the four corners for this exercise on the *One Anothering* facilitator website, *oneanothering.com*. If you are meeting online, we recommend using your fingers to communicate which quadrant you would likely hold.

FACILITATOR

As each situation is read, move to the posture you are likely to inhabit in that situation.

Which posture tends to be your default when:

1. You feel stressed.
2. You feel supported.
3. You feel like someone is treating you with contempt.
4. You feel out of your league.
5. There is pressure to give an immediate answer.
6. You feel defensive.
7. The stakes feel high.
8. You are engaging social media.
9. You are responding to someone who is spreading misinformation.
10. You feel someone is being dishonest with you.

CONVERSING WITH COMPASSION AND CONVICTION *(10 minutes)*

Finally, let's have paired conversations in which we practice holding compassion and conviction together as we discuss the role of the church in politics. Pair up and decide who will represent which position in the conversation: We ask that you each choose a distinct view, even if it isn't the one you resonate with most.

View 1: Pastors and/or the church should speak more directly into our political process.

View 2: Politics should remain separate from the pulpit and/or the church.

Discuss this topic, seeking to hold compassion and conviction together in that conversation.

DISCUSSION

What did it look like when you held compassion and conviction together?

What helped you do so?

What made it hard?

⑤ Closing Prayer: Praise, Lament, Hope *4 minutes*

FACILITATOR Colossians 1:17 reminds us—especially when things are difficult or seem to be falling apart—that Jesus is reconciling all things. Yet, we must face the reality that many things are not as they should be. It is important to name before God and one another what has gone wrong in our hearts, in our communities, and in the world.

This prayer practice invites us to lament what's broken in the context of affirming God's goodness and hoping in God's promises. We will first voice our praises, then our laments, and finally, our hopes.

First, let's voice our **praises**. God, you are good and your love endures forever. For what good gifts do we give thanks to God? What happened in our time together that moves us to praise?

Allow space for the voicing of praises.

Let's move to lament. We know that all is not well in this broken world. How are we disappointed with God, ourselves, and even one another? How does our time together lead us to lament or confess?

Allow space for the voicing of laments.

Finally, let's turn to hope. Because Christ holds all things together, we can look toward the future with hope. What do we hope for and ask God to do?

Allow space for the voicing of hopes.

Now to him who is able to do far more abundantly than all that we ask or think, according to the power at work within us, to him be glory in the church and in Christ Jesus throughout all generations, forever and ever.

Amen.

⑥ Live it Out

1 minute

Briefly review this invitation to live it out before next session.

NOTICING COMPASSION AND CONVICTION
Pay attention to how you and others engage conflict — political or otherwise — this week. Keep a compassion/conviction journal, capturing what you notice about what is said or done. Then, consider which posture each encounter best fits.

SESSION 5
From Rigidity to Humility

OVERVIEW

In this session, we will consider how to shift from rigidity to humility by practicing the habit of getting curious.

OUTLINE

1 Opening Prayer (1 minute)	53
2 Follow Up: Noticing Compassion and Conviction (10 minutes)	55
3 From Rigidity to Humility (20+ minutes)	56
4 Getting Curious (25+ minutes)	58
5 Closing Prayer: Litany of Humility (3 minutes)	60
6 Live it Out (1 minute)	61

(1)

Opening Prayer *5 minutes*

To open our time together, we will read 1 Corinthians 13, considering what it means for political engagement. As you listen to the passage, listen for a word or phrase that catches your attention.

> If I speak in the tongues of mortals or of angels, but do not have love, I am only a resounding gong or a clanging cymbal. If I have the gift of prophecy and can fathom all mysteries and all knowledge, and if I have a faith that can move mountains, but do not have love, I am nothing. If I give all I possess to the poor and give over my body to hardship that I may boast, but do not have love, I gain nothing.
>
> Love is patient, love is kind. It does not envy, it does not boast, it is not proud. It does not dishonor others, it is not self-seeking, it is not easily angered, it keeps no record of wrongs. Love does not delight in evil but rejoices with the truth. It always protects, always trusts, always hopes, always perseveres.
>
> Love never fails. But where there are prophecies, they will cease; where there are tongues, they will be stilled; where there is knowledge, it will pass away. For we know in part and we prophesy in part, but when completeness comes, what is in part disappears. When I was a child, I talked like a child, I thought like a child, I reasoned like a child. When I became an adult, I put the ways of childhood behind me. For now we see only a reflection as in a mirror; then we shall see face to face. Now I know in part; then I shall know fully, even as I am fully known.
>
> And now these three remain: faith, hope and love. But the greatest of these is love.
>
> 1 Corinthians 13

What word or phrase caught your attention?

Let's pray in unison:

GROUP **God of Love,**
We confess that we know only in part,
Although we sometimes speak as though
we know the whole.
We see as in a cloudy mirror,
yet we sometimes act like our vision is perfect.

In these moments we ask for the wisdom
to acknowledge our limitations,
And for the grace to welcome the limitations of others.

May our love be patient and kind,
Humble and honoring of others.
May we protect, trust, hope, and persevere,
As we follow you into unfailing love.

Amen.

(2)

Follow Up: Noticing Compassion and Conviction

10 minutes

Last session, we focused on shifting from cocooning and combat to covenantal communication (refer back to chart on page 45):

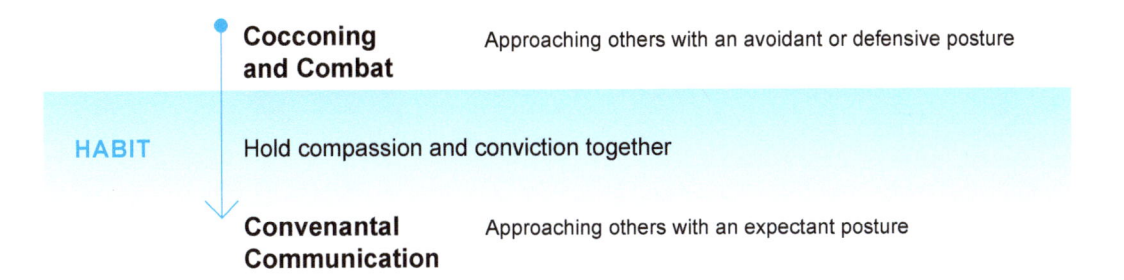

HABIT

Coccooning and Combat — Approaching others with an avoidant or defensive posture

Hold compassion and conviction together

Convenantal Communication — Approaching others with an expectant posture

Respond to the question below as you feel led:

DISCUSSION

What did you notice or wonder as you paid attention to compassion and conviction?

3

From Rigidity to Humility   *20 minutes*

This video introduces a shift from rigidity to humility that will help us participate in politics with a Kingdom posture that reflects love for one another, even as our differences remain.

From Rigidity to Humility

FROM TANNER SMITH

oneanothering.com/politics5 | *4:08*

KEY IDEAS IN THE VIDEO

Jesus repeatedly teaches his followers that those who think highly of themselves will be humbled, and those who embrace humility will be honored.

Paul also ties together humility and love. As Paul invites us to love others—deeply, sacrificially—he reminds us how limited our perspectives are.

Spending time in solitude with God is a spiritual practice that helps us to understand and accept our limitations. It also helps us understand that we need one another, as we each see things others don't.

Getting curious—wondering about what we don't know or understand—helps move us from rigidity to humility. With the Spirit's help, we can move from the posture of a know-it-all, assuming that we already know all that we need to, to instead take the posture of a learner, pursuing truth and discerning what is right and just.

HUMILITY ≠ INDIFFERENCE

We ought to be careful not to confuse humility with indifference. Indifference sounds like, "I don't care about learning more or having an opinion about this. I'm uninterested in digging deeper." Indifference can also look like overwhelm and giving up on the pursuit of truth and justice: "I just don't know what to think!" Notice how this false humility could easily be mistaken for actual humility.

	Rigidity	Arrogant certainty about one's position that closes one off to new information, experiences, or perspectives
HABIT	Get Curious	
	Humility	Being aware of and owning our limitations while pursuing deeper knowledge, truth, and understanding

DISCUSSION

In the video, Tanner contrasted the posture of rigidity and the posture of humility. In this activity, you will explore times when you've observed each of those postures in action in the midst of a political conflict, considering how it looked, the impact it had, and the mindsets and habits that enabled it.

Take five minutes to reflect individually. Then, share your observations with one another.

1. Think of a time when you observed—in yourself or someone else—a rigid posture in relation to a political conflict. What did it look like? What was its impact? What mindsets and habits encourage that way of being in the world?

2. Think of a time when you observed—in yourself or someone else—a humble posture in relation to a political conflict. What did it look like? What was its impact? What mindsets and habits encourage that way of being in the world?

3. What difference does it make in your interactions when someone is humble and listening closely to you? What do you wonder?

4

Getting Curious *30 minutes*

When we engage political conflict from a rigid posture, we are likely to get defensive. We engage differences in order to critique or convince others, without being receptive to learning something new.

When we listen with humility, we get curious, asking questions that stem from a genuine desire to understand. Curious questions (and the tone with which they are asked) should reflect a sincere effort to understand others and their perspectives from their points of view. Getting curious can prompt us to examine ourselves, as well. Curious questions should be relationally attentive, responding to the person, context, and conversation.

Below are some examples of curious questions. Look them over individually and circle three that you would like to get into the habit of asking more often:

SAMPLE CURIOUS QUESTIONS AND PROMPTS

- Would you tell me more about what you mean?
- What is important to you about this?
- How did you come to see it this way?
- What would you like things to look like?
- Tell me more.
- Help me understand . . .
- How does ___ make you feel?
- What concerns you about . . . ?
- Can you put that another way?
- Can you say more about . . . ?
- How does this fit with your values?
- Can you give me an example?
- I'm wondering . . .

INTROSPECTIVE CURIOUS QUESTIONS
Questions to ask yourself when in conversation with others

- What might I have misunderstood about what they said?
- What do I share in common with this person?
- What if what they are saying is true?
- What if I were to assume they are acting reasonably?
- What are the strengths of their view?
- What don't I know?
- What concerns or questions do I have about their view?
- What concerns or questions do I have about my own view?
- What am I learning about my own perspective?

PAIRED PRACTICE

We are now going to practice getting curious while talking about politics in pairs. If there is an odd number of people in your group, you will have one group of three in which a different person observes each round.

When it is your turn to speak, choose one of the sets of political issues below on which to focus:

- Immigration, refugees, protecting borders, sanctuary cities

- American identity, patriotism

- Shootings, terrorism, gun control

- Race, racism, social justice

- Gender, sexuality, sexism

- Censorship, hate speech, political correctness

In your pairs, work through the following steps:

1. Pray Together	May the words of our mouths and the meditations of our hearts be acceptable to you. Amen. (Psalm 19:14)
2. Round 1 *4 minutes*	One person will talk about their perspective on a political issue. The other will get curious.
3. Round 2 *4 minutes*	Switch roles and issues.
4. Debrief *2 minutes*	What did you notice? What do you wonder? What does getting curious make possible?

⑤ Closing Prayer

3 minutes

FACILITATOR O Jesus! meek and humble of heart,

GROUP **Hear me.**

FACILITATOR From the desire of being esteemed, loved, extolled, honored, and praised,

GROUP **Deliver me, Jesus.**

FACILITATOR From the desire of being preferred to others, of being consulted, of being approved,

GROUP **Deliver me, Jesus.**

FACILITATOR From the fear of being humiliated, despised, rebuked, or forgotten,

GROUP **Deliver me, Jesus.**

FACILITATOR From the fear of being ridiculed, wronged, or suspected,

GROUP **Deliver me, Jesus.**

FACILITATOR That others may be loved and esteemed more than I,

GROUP **Jesus, grant me the grace to desire it.**

FACILITATOR That, in the opinion of the world, others may increase and I may decrease,

GROUP **Jesus, grant me the grace to desire it.**

FACILITATOR That others may be chosen and I set aside,

GROUP **Jesus, grant me the grace to desire it.**

FACILITATOR That others may be praised and I unnoticed,

GROUP **Jesus, grant me the grace to desire it.**

FACILITATOR That others may become holier than I, provided that I become as holy as I should,

GROUP **Jesus, grant me the grace to desire it.
Amen.**

(Adapted from Rafael Cardinal Memy de Val (1865-1930), Secretary of State to Pope Pius X)

⑥ Live it Out

1 minute

Briefly review this invitation to live it out before next session.

PRACTICING HUMILITY

Choose a political issue about which you care deeply. Intentionally lean into that issue this week with at least one person who sees it differently. In those conversations, practice humility (being aware of and owning our limitations while pursuing deeper knowledge, truth, and understanding) by getting curious. Use the list of questions above as a resource. Pay attention to what you notice about humility and what getting curious makes possible.

SESSION 6
From Dismissive to Forbearing

OVERVIEW

In this session, we will consider how to shift from dismissing others to forbearing (bearing with) by practicing the habit of gracious differentiation.

OUTLINE

1 Opening Prayer (2 minutes)	63
2 Follow Up: Practicing Humility (10 minutes)	64
3 From Dismissive to Forbearing (20 minutes+)	65
4 Practicing Gracious Differentiation (25 minutes+)	68
5 Closing Prayer: Breath Prayer (7 minutes)	70
6 Live it Out (1 minute)	71

(1)

Opening Prayer　　　　　　　　　　　　　　　　　　　*2 minutes*

FACILITATOR Lord of yesterday, today, tomorrow, and forever, we do not know what lies ahead, and we confess that we want to.

GROUP **We not only want to know, but we want to control. We bring to you our worry, our fear, our frustration, our dismay, and we lay them at your feet.**

FACILITATOR We exchange our certainty for faith, our anxious activity for trusting stillness.

GROUP **We desire forbearance. Fix our eyes again upon your eternal promises.**

FACILITATOR Anchor our hearts and minds in the knowledge that whatever happens, we are yours.

GROUP **We surrender ourselves to you again, echoing the words of our Savior: "Thy will be done."
Amen.**

②

Follow Up: Practicing Humility   *10 minutes*

Last session, we focused on making this shift:

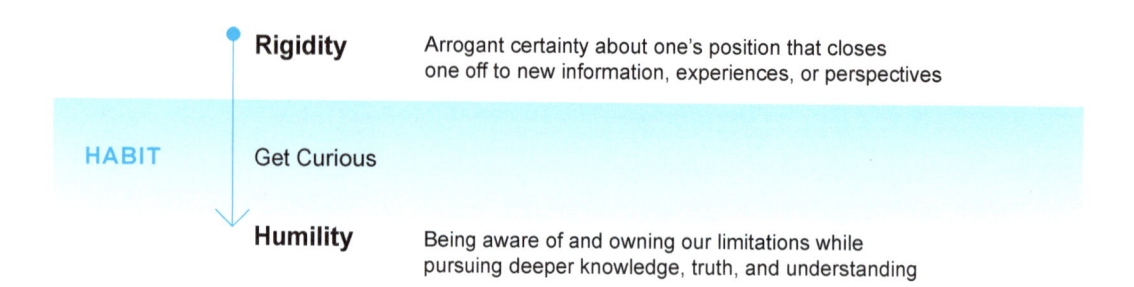

HABIT

- **Rigidity** — Arrogant certainty about one's position that closes one off to new information, experiences, or perspectives
- **Get Curious**
- **Humility** — Being aware of and owning our limitations while pursuing deeper knowledge, truth, and understanding

Respond to the questions below as you feel led:

DISCUSSION

What did you notice about humility
and what getting curious makes possible?

Are there limits to getting curious as a virtuous habit?
Under which circumstances would curiosity
not be the best way to love another?

(3)

From Dismissive to Forbearing   20 minutes

This video introduces a shift from dismissiveness to forbearance that will help us participate in politics with a Kingdom posture that reflects love for one another, even as our differences remain.

From Dismissive to Forbearing

FROM ASHLEE EILAND

oneanothering.com/politics6 | 4:35

KEY IDEAS IN THE VIDEO

Our polarized context is rife with habits that demonstrate impatience with and disregard for those on the "other side" by cutting them out.

Jesus invites us to act instead with forbearance: bearing with one another amidst differences as a reflection of trust in God's grace.

A polarized mindset that fuels disconnection is the belief that forbearance requires giving up our convictions. It is possible to connect with empathy and compassion, even while disagreeing. We differentiate graciously when we are honest about our differences while remaining in relationship.

Dismissive — Disconnecting as a way to manage discomfort or anxiety that we experience related to differences

HABIT — Differentiate Graciously

Forbearing — Bearing with one another amidst differences as a reflection of our trust in God's grace

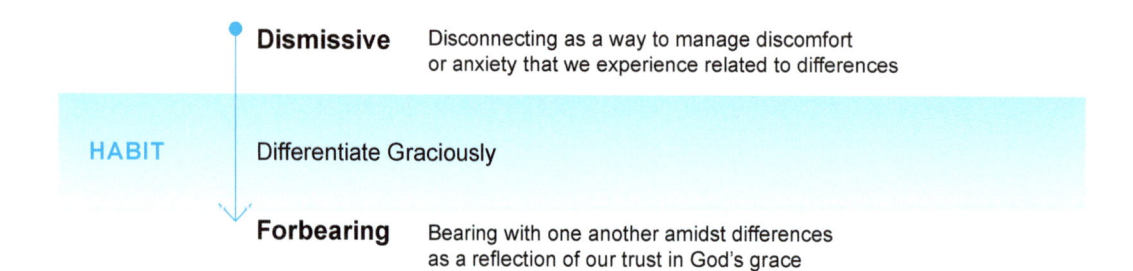

DISCUSSION

Process the video by engaging the following questions. We suggest that you first take five minutes to reflect individually; then discuss in pairs for about five minutes, and finally discuss key insights with the whole group for about five minutes.

GRACIOUS DIFFERENTIATION Being both *connected* and *defined*

BEING CONNECTED	Remaining in relationship
BEING DEFINED	Being clear about your convictions. There are two parts: • Communicating who you are, what you believe, what you want, and what you will (and will not) do, and • Allowing others to do the same

1. Which dismissive habit below is most tempting to you when you experience discomfort or anxiety related to political differences?

DISMISSIVE HABITS	
CUTTING OUT	Being defined but disconnected
CAVING	Being connected but not defining oneself
CONTROLLING	Being connected but not allowing others to define themselves

Describe what that habit looks like for you as well as what leads you to respond in that way.

2. What examples of differentiating graciously have you observed or experienced in political conversations?

4

Practicing Gracious Differentiation   *20 minutes*

When someone says something we disagree with or have concerns about, there are many ways we might disconnect from the other person in that moment. In this exercise, you will have two rounds of conversation, each three minutes long. In the first round, you will enact disconnected responses. In the second round, you will enact gracious responses.

STEP 1: FORM GROUPS OF THREE
Decide which person will play Role A. The other two people will work together to play Role B. Each round of conversation will be three minutes long.

Role A: Be yourself and share your thoughts in response to this prompt:

What most matters to you in either local or national politics?

Role B: Role play in response to what the other person says, enacting either disconnected or gracious responses, depending on the round. Before you begin, review the types of responses related to that round (see next page).

STEP 2: ENGAGE IN CONVERSATION
Round 1: Disconnected Responses

Round 2: Gracious Responses

STEP 3: DEBRIEF
Remain in your small group to discuss the following questions for three minutes:
- Which habits for responding to differences do I want to leave behind?

- Which habits for responding to differences do I want to carry with me?

STEP 4: RECONVENE AS A GROUP
Invite individuals to share insights they had with the group.

ROUND 1: DISCONNECTED RESPONSES

Responses that express rejection of the other and undermine connection.

Disconnected Responses	Description
Ignoring	Not acknowledging what is said or pretending someone didn't say something
Interrupting	Cutting off another person while they are speaking through words or actions
Irrelevant	Responding in ways that are unrelated to what was said such as changing the subject or responding with well-worn talking points
Impersonal	Guarded communication that stays at the level of clichés or jargon
Incoherent	Responding by rambling
Inconsistent	Responding verbally in ways that contradict your nonverbal communication
Insincere	Pretending you agree when you do not
Unsupportive	Denying or discounting their feelings or experience
Presumptuous	Engaging in ways that presume that others hold the same views you do

ROUND 2: GRACIOUS RESPONSES

Responses that express valuing the other person and build connection. Agreement is only one way to do this. We can recognize and acknowledge one another while disagreeing.

Gracious Responses	Description
Directly Acknowledging	Reacting directly to what was said
Prompting	Offering a small nudge to encourage the person to say more
Supporting	Expressing care, empathy, and interest
Reflecting	Mirroring what you heard back to the person
Clarifying	Seeking to better understand what was said
Agreeing about Content	Reinforcing what was said (if genuinely felt)
Expressing a Positive Feeling	Expressing positive emotions about what was said (if genuinely felt)
Inviting	Interacting in ways that make room for differences

These two charts are adapted from Sarah Trenholm and Arthur Jensen, Interpersonal Communication. They are drawing upon research from Frank E. X. Dance and Carl E. Larson, Speech Communication, Concepts and Behavior.

(5)

Closing Prayer: Breath Prayer *7 minutes*

In order to practice gracious differentiation, we have to pay attention to the discomfort and anxiety we experience that can lead us to cut off, cave, or control. When we notice pressure mounting, returning to a memorized or repeated prayer can slow us down and anchor us in Christ.

The same science that helps athletes transform their stress also stands behind the ancient spiritual practice of Breath Prayer. Breathing can reignite an intimacy with the One who is closer to us than our very breath. The linguistic connection between spirit and breath is unambiguous in the Bible: Both the Hebrew *ruach* and Greek *pneuma* mean breath, wind, and/or spirit.

As we enter a time of silent prayer, let's each choose one of the breath prayers listed below or a favorite we already use:

1. In you, Oh God, I put my trust.
2. Be still and know that I am God.
3. You are my refuge and my strength.
4. I find rest in your shelter.
5. I won't be afraid for you are with me.
6. Lead me, Lord; I will follow.
7. O Lord, come to my assistance; O God make haste to help me.
8. Jesus, let me feel your love (or power, strength, etc.).

Let's take a few minutes to silently pray, syncing the prayer with our breaths:

1. Sit quietly. Feel the rhythm of your breath. Become aware of God's presence.
2. Pray the first half on the inhale and the second on the exhale, uniting your prayer with your body and breath.
3. Enjoy the peace and security that come from resting in God's arms.

When the heat of conflict rises, returning to this Breath Prayer can anchor us in Christ and remind us of God's faithfulness. Slowing down and rooting in Christ invites a forbearing posture and encourages differentiating graciously rather than dismissiveness.

6

Live it Out   *1 minute*

Briefly review this invitation to live it out before next session.

GRACIOUS DIFFERENTIATION

Think of a situation or relationship where your anxiety is high and pay attention to that situation or relationship between now and the next session:

- Pay attention to times when it seems that others feel they have to go along with you in order to maintain relationship. How can you invite others to define themselves?
- Pay attention to times when you give in to others in order to avoid friction. How can you define yourself clearly and courageously?
- Pay attention to times when you are tempted to cut someone out. How can you stay connected?

Turn to page 73 for prep work to complete prior to Session 7.

Pray for one another.

James 5:16

Preparation for Session 7

Complete before next session

To facilitate going deep on a political issue, indicate the extent to which you agree with each of the statements below.

	Strongly Disagree	Disagree	Neither Agree nor Disagree	Agree	Strongly Agree
1. Families trapped in underperforming schools have much to gain from school voucher programs.					
2. The US government is extremely inefficient.					
3. While we rightly care how tax money is spent, I shouldn't insist that my tax money be used for my own direct benefit.					
4. Politicians on the left and right are equally misguided in preserving their own power rather than serving the American people.					
5. The government is doing too many things that would be better left to businesses and individuals.					
6. Public school teachers are hard-working individuals seeking to provide quality education with too little funding.					
7. Most corporations make a fair and reasonable amount of profit.					
8. Initiatives led by the government are more accountable to the public than those led by private businesses.					
9. It is the responsibility of the federal government to make sure all Americans have health care coverage.					
10. Undocumented immigrants should be required to return to their own country.					
11. This country should do whatever it takes to protect the environment.					
12. Abortion should be illegal in most cases.					
13. When voters in the U.S. hold different religions and speak different languages, it strengthens and improves American culture and identity.					
14. The economic system in this country is generally fair to most Americans.					

SESSION 7
From Reticence to Courage

OVERVIEW

In this session, we will consider how to shift from reticence (or hesitance) to courage by practicing the habit of going deep.

OUTLINE

1 Opening Prayer (5 minutes)	75
2 Follow Up: Gracious Differentiation (10 minutes)	77
3 From Reticence to Courage (15+ minutes)	78
4 Go Deep with Yourself (10+ minutes)	80
5 Go Deep Together (15 minutes)	82
6 Closing Prayer (3 minutes)	83
7 Live it Out (1 minute)	84

(1)

Opening Prayer: Palms Down, Palms Up   *5 minutes*

FACILITATOR   Today we are going to return to the prayer practice we did in the first session: Palms Down, Palms Up. This practice invites us to surrender to God and receive from God.

Let's begin with these words from Psalm 27:

GROUP   **The Lord is my light and my salvation—
whom shall I fear?
The Lord is the stronghold of my life—
of whom shall I be afraid?** (Psalm 27:1)

FACILITATOR   Let's place our palms down, in an emptying posture. Placing our palms down reflects our desire to turn over any concerns we may have to God. As we pray, we surrender what we usually grasp and cling to.

Let's pray aloud, naming things that we wish to release as we begin our time together as a group. For example, "Lord, I surrender my anxiety about talking about politics." "I release my fear of silence to you."

Whatever weighs on our minds or hearts or is a concern, let's release it to God.

Allow space for spoken or silent prayers

Please join me in these words from Psalm 27:

GROUP   **Teach me your way, Lord;
lead me in a straight path** (Psalm 27:11a)

FACILITATOR   Now let's place our palms up, in a receiving posture. Placing our palms up is a symbol of our desire to receive from God.

Let's pray aloud, asking God to provide for us. For example, "Lord, give me peace about this conversation." "Lord, give us hope for how we might participate in politics."

Whatever we need, let's ask God to provide it.

Allow space for spoken or silent prayers

Let's close by saying these words from Psalm 27:

GROUP   **Wait for the Lord;
be strong and take heart
and wait for the Lord.** (Psalm 27:14)
Amen.

(2)

Follow Up: Gracious Differentiation *10 minutes*

Last session, we focused on making this shift:

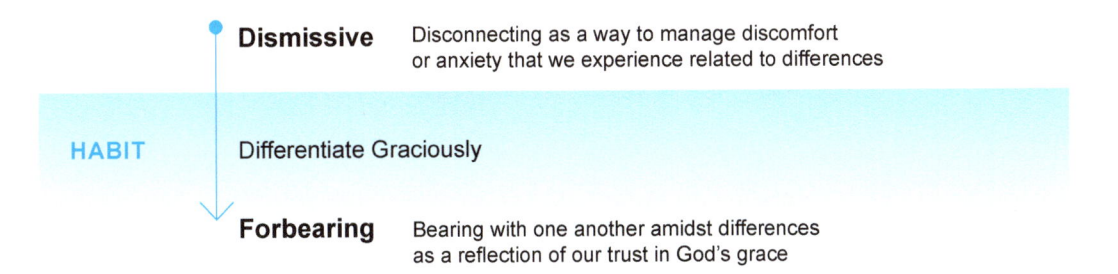

Dismissive — Disconnecting as a way to manage discomfort or anxiety that we experience related to differences

HABIT — Differentiate Graciously

Forbearing — Bearing with one another amidst differences as a reflection of our trust in God's grace

Respond to the question below as you feel led:

DISCUSSION

What did you notice or wonder as you paid attention to gracious differentiation in a particular situation or relationship?

3

From Reticence to Courage *15 minutes*

This video introduces a shift from reticence (or hesitance) to courage that will help us participate in politics with a Kingdom posture that reflects love for one another, even as our differences remain.

From Reticence to Courage
FROM ASHLEE EILAND

oneanothering.com/politics7 | 4:37

KEY IDEAS IN THE VIDEO
Courage is acting despite fear. We build courage by surrendering control and experiencing the faithfulness of God.

One way to practice courage in the midst of political conflict is to risk going deep, moving beyond what's visible above the surface to understand what lies beneath.

When we go deep with ourselves, we grow in self-awareness and have the opportunity to re-form our mindsets, hopes, fears, and loves when we find that they are out of alignment with God's Kingdom. When we invite others into the depths with us through courageous sharing, we demonstrate gracious differentiation.

When we go deep with others through courageous listening, we grow in understanding and affection. We might even discover shared hopes and loves that provide ways to work together despite the very real differences that remain.

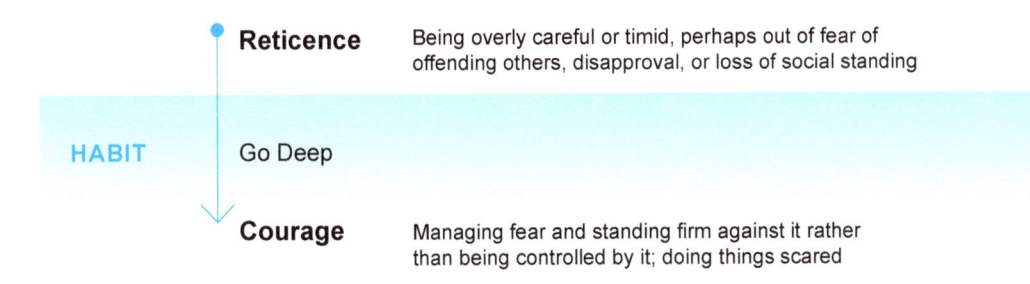

	Reticence	Being overly careful or timid, perhaps out of fear of offending others, disapproval, or loss of social standing
HABIT	Go Deep	
	Courage	Managing fear and standing firm against it rather than being controlled by it; doing things scared

DISCUSSION

Process the video by engaging the following questions as a group:

1. When is a time when you exercised courage in relation to politics? What helped you be courageous?

2. Why is courage important for engaging politics with a Kingdom posture? What does courage do?

3. Why is courage essential for practicing gracious differentiation (being both connected and defined)?

4

Go Deep with Yourself

10 minutes

Going deep—moving beyond what's visible to understand what lies beneath—is one way to practice courage. To enter the depths, we start by identifying a strong emotion and seek to understand what lies below that response. When we are angry about something, for example, it typically reflects a fear that we have. Identifying that fear can point us to something we dearly love that we are seeking to protect. By going beneath what we see or experience on the surface, we better understand what's at stake for us and our strong response.

1. Spend five minutes going deep individually, guided by the prompts below:

   Breaking Ground: Anger
   Identify a political issue or policy to which you react strongly. Perhaps it leads you to feel angry or resentful. What is the issue or policy? Describe how it makes you feel.

   Digging Deeper: Fear
   Seek to understand what is beneath your strong reaction. What are you concerned might go wrong? Who are you concerned may be harmed? What might be lost?

   Finding Treasure: Love
   What do you love that is under threat? What or whom are your fears seeking to protect? How does your strong reaction connect with your deep loves?

2. Reconvene as a group, inviting individuals to share insights they had with the group.

What we say

Emotions we express

Positions on issues

Mindsets

Hopes

Loves

Fears

⑤ Go Deep Together

15 minutes

STEP 1: PREPARATION

Return to page 73 that you completed between last session and now.

STEP 2: PAIRED CONVERSATION

1. Find a partner and identify one issue where your responses diverge in the chart on page 73. We will engage that issue in two rounds of conversation.

2. Have a three-minute conversation in which one person courageously shares their perspective and the mindsets, hopes, fears, and loves beneath the surface. The other person should courageously listen, resisting the desire to explain or defend their own position, focusing instead on developing a deeper understanding of their partner. If helpful, the courageous listener can ask questions like those to the right.

    QUESTIONS FOR GOING DEEP
    - What's at stake in this for you?
    - What do we lose when we get this wrong?
    - What needs protecting?
    - What shared loves can we identify?

3. Switch roles and have a second three-minute conversation.

4. Discuss the following questions with your partner:
    - What did you notice about your thoughts and feelings as you courageously spoke? As you courageously listened?
    - In what ways did you encourage one another?
    - How does practicing courage by going deep challenge you?
    - What does practicing courage by going deep make possible?

STEP 3: GROUP DEBRIEFING

Reconvene as a group, inviting individuals to share insights they had with the group.

6

Closing Prayer　　　　　　　　　　　　　　　　*3 minutes*

GROUP	**Lord,**
Our wounds and worries often undermine our courage.

Give us the courage to listen,
Open us to connection and understanding,
To lean in, and learn,
to ask, to consider,
to sit awhile with discomfort.

Give us the courage to speak up,
Form us to demonstrate both conviction and compassion.
To lean in, and learn,
to speak, to consider,
to sit awhile with discomfort.

We are in search of You,
and yearn for your Kingdom.
May your Presence fill us,
And your Spirit lead us,
to know and be known by one another.

Amen

(7)

Live it Out

1 minute

Briefly review this invitation to live it out before next session.

PRACTICING COURAGE
Choose a political issue about which you care deeply (a different one from two sessions ago).

This week, intentionally lean into that issue with at least one person who sees it differently.

In those conversations, practice courage by

- Going deep both as a courageous listener and a courageous speaker.

- Pay attention to what you notice about courage and what going deep makes possible.

Build up one another.

Romans 14:19

Polarized Politics	Scarcity	Contempt	Cocooning & Combat	Rigidity	Dismissive	Reticence	**Despair**
Kingdom Politics	Abundance	Love	Covenantal Communication	Humility	Forebearing	Courage	**Hope**

SESSION 8
From Despair to Hope

OVERVIEW

In this session, we will consider how to shift from despair to hope by practicing the habit of waiting expectantly.

OUTLINE

1 Opening Prayer (2 minutes)	87
2 Follow Up: Practicing Courage (10 minutes)	88
3 From Despair to Hope (10+ minutes)	89
4 Inviting the Spirit to Transform Us (28+ minutes)	91
5 Closing Prayer: Praise, Lament, Hope (8+ minutes)	94
6 Closing Invitation (2 minutes)	95

1

Opening Prayer *2 minutes*

GROUP
**How, O Lord, can we have hope
when this world is such an insecure place?
Natural calamities destroy.
Economic uncertainties abound.
Human beings kill.**

FACILITATOR Jesus says, I am the light of the world.

GROUP
**What, O God, is reliable? What is secure?
Not people.
Not institutions.
Not governments.**

FACILITATOR Jesus says, I am the way, the truth, and the life.

GROUP
**We fear, Lord, that evil will win out in the end.
We worry that our efforts will be for nothing.**

FACILITATOR Jesus says, I am the resurrection and the life.

GROUP
You alone, O Lord, are our hope. You alone are our safety. You alone are our strength. May we—even with our fears and anxieties, our insecurities and uncertainties—swing like needles to the pole star of the Spirit.

Amen.

②

Follow Up: Practicing Courage   *10 minutes*

Last session, we focused on making this shift:

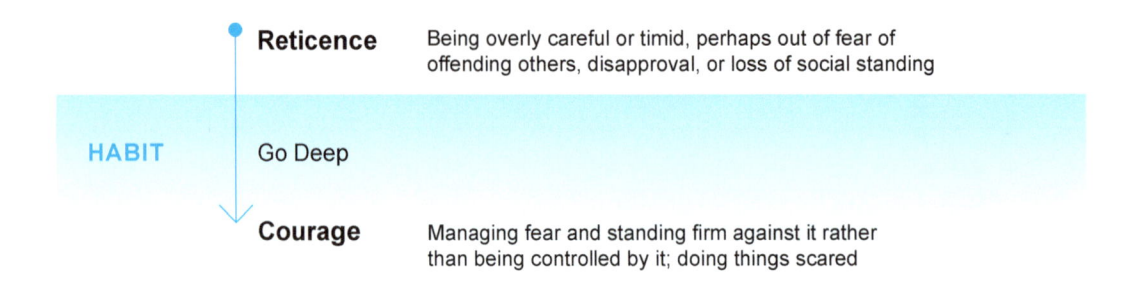

	Reticence	Being overly careful or timid, perhaps out of fear of offending others, disapproval, or loss of social standing
HABIT	Go Deep	
	Courage	Managing fear and standing firm against it rather than being controlled by it; doing things scared

Respond to the question below as you feel led:

DISCUSSION

What did you notice or wonder as you practiced going deep both as a courageous listener and a courageous speaker?

(3)

From Despair to Hope
10 minutes

This video introduces a shift from despair to hope that will help us participate in politics with a Kingdom posture that reflects love for one another, even as our differences remain.

From Despair to Hope
FROM TANNER SMITH

oneanothering.com/politics8 | 4:29

KEY IDEAS IN THE VIDEO

Political polarization tempts us to give in to despair and disengage because we feel like there's nothing we can do.

A Kingdom posture requires hope: Believing in God's goodness and trusting that God is making all things new, even when circumstances tell a different story.

Hope asks, "What are you waiting for?" and, "What will you do while you wait?"

In Matthew 25, Jesus tells a story about hope as waiting expectantly. The wise women prepared by bringing extra oil for their lamps. The foolish women didn't prepare.

God invites us to keep our eyes and ears prepared for God's Kingdom breaking out all around us and to join in by aligning our hearts, our minds, and our hands with the vision God lays out. The Kingdom of God isn't simply a distant future for which we long, it is a way of life that we get to participate in—even, and especially, in our politics.

● **Despair**   Assuming that nothing can be done

HABIT   Wait Expectantly

Hope   Believing in God's goodness and trusting that God is making all things new

DISCUSSION

Process the video by engaging the following questions as a group for five minutes.

1. How has our time together expanded our understanding of what might be possible?

2. How has our time together helped us consider what we might do while we wait?

(4)

Inviting the Spirit to Transform Us *28 minutes*

In this time of prayerful reflection and sharing, we will consider the posture for engaging political differences that we long for the Spirit to form in us. While we acknowledge that our formation is only possible through the Spirit's power, we recognize that we also have a role to play.

POSTURE		MINDSET		HABITS
Way of being	=	Way of thinking	+	Ways of interacting

STEP 1: INDIVIDUAL REFLECTION ON OUR POSTURES

Spend a few minutes reflecting individually about the posture that you desire to hold as you engage political differences. How do you want others to experience you? How would you want them to describe you? Describe your desired posture here:

STEP 2: SHARE OUR REFLECTIONS ABOUT OUR POSTURES
Let's share our desired postures, going around the circle, giving each person a chance to briefly share (in a sentence, not a paragraph). Please resist the temptation to affirm, comment, or build on each other's ideas in order to allow each person's experience to be shared and received as equally relevant and valuable.

STEP 3: GROUP DISCUSSION
Briefly discuss as a group: What mindsets are important for enabling our desired postures? How might shifting our mindsets from scarcity to abundance and contempt to love be important for enabling our desired ways of being?

STEP 4: INDIVIDUAL REFLECTION ON OUR HABITS
Now, spend five minutes prayerfully reflecting on your habits. You might consider various habits, such as:

- Everyday rhythms (e.g., your commuting routine)
- Spiritual practices (e.g., prayer, Scripture engagement)
- Communication patterns (e.g., thinking of a response rather than listening)
- Media consumption (e.g., checking the news often, scrolling social media)
- Political engagement (e.g., staying silent)

What habits do you want God to help you...

...Stop: Which of your current habits undermine the posture you desire?

...Continue: Which of your current habits support the posture you desire?

...Start: What new habits might help you develop the posture you desire?

STEP 5: SHARE OUR REFLECTIONS ON OUR HABITS
Let's each share one habit we want to stop and one habit we want to start in a Go Round: We will go around the circle, giving each person a chance to briefly share.

STEP 6: PRAY TOGETHER
Ultimately, it is the Holy Spirit who forms us. Let's close this conversation by asking the Spirit to sanctify us:

> **Come, Holy Spirit, remind us of your great mercy.**
> **Make our listening, speaking, and doing**
> **Holy and pleasing to you.**
> **Transform us by the renewing of our minds,**
> **so that we can seek your will.**
> **And may we live as one body,**
> **belonging to one another,**
> **as we belong to you. Amen.**

5

Closing Prayer: Praise, Lament, Hope   *8 minutes*

As we wrap up this final session, we'll reflect not only on how things went during this session, but how things have gone throughout this small group. Take a minute to reflect silently. Write down one praise, one lament, and one hope.

PRAISE What is praiseworthy?

LAMENT What needs to be lamented?

HOPE What hopes do we have?

We encourage you to gather in a circle for this time of prayer.

FACILITATOR Let's share our praises, laments, and hopes in a time of prayer. We start with praise. What do we give thanks to God for? Just call out a phrase or sentence.

Allow space for the voicing of praises.

Now let's voice our laments. What are we sad about? What do we wish was different? We can share these things honestly with God and one another.

Allow space for the voicing of laments.

Finally, we look to the future. What do we hope for?

Allow space for the voicing of hopes.

GROUP **Lord, hear our prayer. Amen.**

THANK YOU FOR PARTICIPATING IN ONE ANOTHERING!

We would be very grateful if you would take the time to fill out a short survey to provide us with feedback.

Be kind and compassionate to one another.

Ephesians 4:32

(6)

Closing Invitation — 2 minutes

Briefly review this invitation to live it out

MY POLITICAL POSTURE
Write a letter to a child you care about, explaining the posture you aspire to hold as you engage in politics and why you seek to engage politics in that way.

In addition to sharing the letter with the child to whom it is addressed (with permission from a parent), consider sending it to members of your small group. The Colossian Forum would also be grateful to receive a copy of your letter: Please email it to programming@colossianforum.org

Glossary

Abundance Mindset: An abundance mindset is believing that God is doing more than we are aware. Someone with an abundance mindset might expect the best from others, assume that God is always giving good gifts, and operate out of a desire to participate in what God is doing in the world.

Behold: To "behold" another person is the practice of seeing others with the eyes of love. It often manifests in seeing the best in others, noticing their value and worth, seeking to understand them, and assuming positive intent in their words and actions.

Breath Prayer: Breath Prayer is a Christian practice where one unites their breath with their body while praying. With each inhale, one part of Scripture or a prayer is silently prayed, and with each exhale, another part of Scripture or a prayer is silently prayed.

Cave: When we "cave," it means we are connected but are not defining ourselves in a conversation or relationship. Examples of caving are not having a sense of self, people-pleasing, and letting go of one's beliefs in order to avoid conflict.

Cocoon: When we "cocoon," we approach disagreement with an avoidant posture. We cocoon by organizing our lives so that we encounter those who see things the way we do and by avoiding conversations about differences with those with whom we disagree.

Combat: When we are in "combat" mode, we approach disagreement with a defensive and/or aggressive posture that seeks to persuade others of why we are right while critiquing other points of view. We listen not to understand but to form a strong response or to find flaws.

Compassion: Compassion refers to approaching others with empathy and generosity rather than disdain and suspicion. A compassionate posture beholds others as made in God's image.

Connected: Being connected means remaining in relationship. Some examples of being connected include: mirroring what you heard back to the person to show you're listening, asking curious questions to better understand what someone is saying, and using body language that is open and encourages the person to say more.

Contempt: Contempt is "a habit of seeing people who disagree with us not as merely incorrect or misguided but as worthless" (Arthur Brooks). Contempt combines anger with disgust or strong dislike for others. Someone who is contemptuous might seek to belittle or dismiss those with a different view than them.

Control: When we control, we are connected but do not allow others to define themselves. Examples of control are remaining in relationship with people but only on your terms and not allowing others to express their own opinions or beliefs.

Courage: Courage is managing fear and standing firm against it rather than being controlled by it. Courage is doing things scared.

Covenant: Covenant refers to a promise made between God and God's people. It can also be a promise made between people in scripture. The concept of covenant is deeply rooted in the biblical narrative, specifically in the Old Testament where God promises to be in covenant with Abraham. In this covenant, God promises to bless Abraham and his descendants and to never stop pursuing and loving them.

Covenantal Communication: Covenantal Communication is a way of being that seeks to emulate God's endless pursuit of and love for God's people in our relationships with one another. Covenantal communication means engaging others from a posture of love and openness, modeling the ways Jesus engages others and honoring the ways God is working in our relationships.

Conviction: Conviction refers to deeply held beliefs, oftentimes based on scripture, life experiences, and worldview. A convicted posture courageously and humbly pursues truth and justice.

Cut-Off: When we "cut-off," we are defined but disconnected. An example of cutting off is leaving a relationship when there are disagreements without openness for further discussion.

Defined: Being defined means being clear about your convictions. Being defined has two parts: 1) Communicating who you are, what you believe, what you want, and what you will (and will not) do; and 2) allowing others to do the same.

Despair: To despair is to disengage because we feel like there's nothing we can do.

Differentiation: Differentiation is when we are honest about our differences while remaining in relationship with one another. It manifests as an individual being able to both hold clear convictions and remain in relationship with others who think, believe, and act differently than them.

Disengagement: Disengagement is giving up and checking out of politics when things get hard and differences arise.

Dismissive: When one is dismissive, one disconnects from others as a way to manage discomfort or anxiety that they experience related to differences or disagreements.

Examine our Political Formation: Examining our political formation involves considering how our beliefs and behaviors related to politics have been shaped and molded by our relationships, experiences, and contexts.

Forbearance: Forbearance means bearing with one another amidst differences as a reflection of God's grace. Forbearance looks like committing to remaining in relationship over time and despite our differences, resisting the pressure for immediate resolution to conflicts, remaining relationally attentive when things are emotionally charged, and offering forgiveness when things go wrong.

Fruit of the Spirit: The "Fruit of the Spirit" are characteristics formed in those who know and live by the Holy Spirit. The fruits of the Spirit are love, joy, peace, patience, kindness, goodness, faithfulness, gentleness, and self-control (Galatians 5:22-23).

Get Curious: To Get Curious is to be receptive to that which we don't know or understand, often by asking curious questions.

Go Deep: Going Deep is a way of being courageous by moving beyond what's visible to understand what lies beneath the surface. Going deeper starts by identifying a strong emotion in yourself or someone else and seeking to understand the fears and loves below that response.

God's Image: Sometimes referred to as the "imago dei," God's Image refers to the concept that human beings were made in the likeness of God. Human beings reflect their Creator. Each human being reflects unique aspects of God's love and character.

Gracious: When one is gracious, one treats others with empathy and compassion, following Christ's example of grace.

Gracious Differentiation: Gracious differentiation is when we are honest about our differences while remaining in a relationship. We can recognize and value another while disagreeing with them.

Habit: Habits are ways of interacting with the world around us that have been learned over time and have become ingrained through repetition.

Hold Compassion and Conviction Together: When we hold compassion and conviction together, we follow the way of Jesus by pursuing truth and love simultaneously. Holding compassion and conviction together means seeking truth and justice in ways that reflect love for both neighbors and enemies.

Hope: Hope is believing in God's goodness and trusting that God is making all things new, even when circumstances tell a different story. Hope asks "What are you waiting for?" and "What will you do while you wait?"

Humility: Humility is being aware of and owning our limitations while pursuing deeper knowledge, truth, and understanding. Humility takes the posture of a learner, pursuing truth and discerning what is right and just.

Indifference: Indifference is false humility that can easily be confused with humility. Indifference sounds like, "I don't care about learning more or having an opinion about this. I'm uninterested in digging deeper." Indifference can also look like overwhelm and giving up on the pursuit of truth and justice: "I just don't know what to think!"

Kingdom of God: Throughout his ministry, Jesus talks about the "kingdom" of God, inviting people to live in it, promising it as an inheritance, preaching that it is already here and is still coming. "Kingdom," however, does not refer to a literal kingdom on earth, but it represents an image of hope for the restoration of all relationships between humankind, God, and creation.

Kingdom Politics: Kingdom politics is participating in community decision-making in ways that align with the teachings and values that God offers us in scripture; for example, enacting Jesus' command to love your enemies and pray for those who persecute you (Matthew 5:44).

Lament: To lament is to express sorrow or anguish to God. Throughout history, communities have engaged the practice of lament to mourn and grieve injustice and suffering. We can lament as individuals or communities for pain in our own context, or we can lament in order to empathize with the pain of others.

Memorable Messages: Memorable messages are sticky messages that influenced our belief systems and behaviors.

Mindset: Mindset refers to a way of thinking about what is and what could be.

Polarization: Polarization is the growing separation between groups of people who hold contrasting beliefs. Polarization might look like increased hostility and unwillingness to seek compromise or understanding of the other.

Polarized Politics: Polarized politics is seen in participating in community decision-making in ways that don't align with the teachings and values that God offers us in scripture; for example, enacting love for neighbor and hate for enemies (Matthew 5:43).

Politics: The term "politics," in its broadest sense, is the navigation of decisions between a community of people. The word "politics" comes from the Greek word for "city." Cities are places where people live together, and living together means making difficult choices about how to share resources, work together, and organize life. Whether at the local or national level, politics often requires finding partial solutions to intractable problems.

Posture: In this context, posture refers to more than just someone's physical stance. One's posture, in a metaphorical sense, refers to one's heart towards and mindset about others. For example, you can have a posture of openness or hostility towards another person.

Reconciliation: Reconciliation is the active pursuit of healing what has been broken. In this context, it's the restoration of relationships that have experienced disrepair in conflict and disagreement. It's a commitment to hearing and understanding one another, even when there are major differences.

Reticence: To be reticent means to be overly careful or timid, perhaps out of fear of offending others, disapproval, or loss of social standing. Someone with a "reticent" attitude may be cautious or hesitant to express themselves fully or engage differences because they are afraid of causing conflict in relationships.

Rigidity: Rigidity is arrogant certainty about one's position that closes one off to new information, experiences, or perspectives. Rigidity takes the posture of a know-it-all, assuming that we already know all that there is to know.

Scarcity Mindset: A scarcity mindset is believing that there is not enough to go around. Someone with a scarcity mindset might assume the worst in people, assume that resources are limited, and operate out of self-interest.

Surrender: Surrender means to give up control of one's desires and one's own need to be right in order to fully hear and accept God's guidance and to strengthen relationships with others in an effort to more fully love God and love others (Matthew 22:36-40).

Virtues: Virtues are highly valued Christian "ways of being" such as hope, humility, generosity, forbearance, and courage. Christian tradition approaches virtues as character traits that one can acquire, with the Spirit's help, through repeated training exercises. Just as a pianist cultivates the skill of playing music by practicing scales, virtue development takes time, practice, and coaching.

Wait Expectantly: To Wait Expectantly is to align one's heart, mind, and hand with the vision God lays out by looking for where the Spirit is at work and actively participating in what the Spirit is doing. Waiting Expectantly reflects the belief that God is at work in the world, that God's Kingdom is breaking out all around us, and that we have an active role to play in it.

Notes

Milton Keynes UK
Ingram Content Group UK Ltd.
UKHW050100070824
446646UK00003B/27